TO EDIFY, HEAL, AND BLESS

The author provides the contents of this book in good faith to encourage, enlighten, and heal. He believes that when the subject discussed is followed, it will produce healing, divine intervention, and miracles from God. However, he does not intend his revelations to take the place of professional counseling and suggestions in your life. Neither is the teaching in this book supposed to be a doctrine to alter your faith in Christ. The author is sure and believes you will be blessed reading this book. However, he will bear no responsibility for any adverse consequences from any wrong understanding and application of the subject taught in this book.

He prays, though, that you will make good use of the teaching and increase your faith in God.

FOLLOW US ON FACEBOOK

Like our page on Facebook for updates:

This title and others are available for quantity discount for sale promotion, gifts, and evangelism. Visit our Facebook page or email us to get started.

All texts, calls, letters, testimonies, and inquiries are welcome.

TABLE OF CONTENTS.

ACKNOWLEDGEMENTS.

An important personality to be acknowledged each time I put pen on paper in attempts to write anything, is the Holy Spirit because He is the one who inspires me to write. His inspiration is unprecedented and incomparable with any existing or previously existed individual who has inspired and encouraged me in such manner. He literarily dictated to me most of the chosen words, sentences, and statements which I write down; and also quickly remembers the scripture which says, "….my tongue is the pen of a ready writer." Actually, He dictates to me most of the sentences, that is why I am even surprised when I come back to read most of these sentences I will be wondering if really I was the one that reasoned out these statements or sentences.

Earlier I was convinced, but today I am double sure it is the Holy Spirit that makes the construction of sentences and statements; I am just the clerk or secretary who penned them down. No wonder the book of Revelation was credited to Christ Jesus, though it was John the Apostle who wrote down the entire revelations. Truly, we learn every day. Without the help of the Holy Spirit nothing would have been written here for your consumption as it were. So, I duly give the entire acknowledgement of this book "Power against drinkers of BLOOD" to Him and Him alone.

Lord Jesus Christ, Holy Spirit, and Father, please take all the glory, exaltations, and magnification, for they duly belong unto you; let no man share the glory with you, Amen. I will not fail also to give thanks to the lord and the Holy Spirit for the immense contributions of Computer Engineers Uche Ihekaire and Gabriel Idisi; their advisory roles are immeasurable. May the good lord reward them accordingly, in Jesus mighty name, amen.

PREFACE.

Satan and his cohorts hate you with perfect hatred. Co-incidentally, Satan the devil does not hide this hatred and wickedness from you and me. Nowadays, these eaters of flesh and drinkers of blood have developed more potent and dangerous methods to operate in the world today. There are certain demonic agents who voluntarily admitted that they eat human flesh and as well drink human blood. They manipulate people and cause their deaths at will, as if they are chickens, goats or dogs.

The speed at which human beings are being spiritually killed or destroyed even in day light is alarming and fearsome. This is the time you must do something to curb the situation; exhibition of a holy anger is advised. You must arise and speak, enough is enough. The eaters of flesh must eat their own flesh, if they must eat flesh, and drink their own blood, if they must drink human blood. This book contains few potential prayer points which will empower you to overcome, demobilize the enemy, and stop the high rate of premature deaths everywhere and in our churches, communities, and our families most especially.

If you follow and obey the simple rules of this book, you will be able to change your flesh and blood to become poison, and you will be too strong for the enemy to tackle. Let us confess this scripture together,

"But thus saith the lord, even the captives of the mighty shall be taken away, and the prey of terrible shall be delivered, for I will contend with him that contendeth with thee, and I will save thy children. And I will feed them that oppress thee with their own flesh; and they shall be drunken with their own blood as with sweet wine: and all flesh shall that I the lord am thy savior and thy redeemer, the mighty one of Jacob." - Isaiah 49:25, 26 – KJV.

And now, in the New Testament it's made far simpler for you to dislodge and vacate your enemy. He said, if you just believe in the name of Jesus Christ, Satan and his cohorts will become a walk-over. Jesus proclaimed in John 6: 47, 53, 54, 56,

"Verily, verily, I say to you, he that believeth on me hath everlasting life. ...Except ye eat the flesh of the son of man, and drink His blood, ye have no life in you, Whoso eateth my flesh and drink my blood, hath eternal life; and I will raise him up at the last day. He that eateth my flesh and drinketh my blood dwelleth in me and I in him."

Do you understand the above scripture? Could this really be true? Yes! This statement is true. As we progressed, you shall have to pray some violent prayers to defeat your enemy and bring him to total submission to the superior power of Christ Jesus.

INTRODUCTION

This few worded write-up is a prayer book specially packaged to address some vital aspects of young Christian's live that are ignorant of so many manipulations of the devil against him or her despite the born-again experience. Imagine where you are still fornicating after becoming born-again or still stealing your relations money and properties or other heinous evil practices, or you still commit adultery against your conscience, or you find yourself routinely living another life under the water with a husband and children, or having sexual intercourse in the dreams. You discovered that you are a witch.

Well, these are the problems you and many other people face, but you can't break free from these evil occurrences; you need someone to help you. Yes, the blood of Jesus Christ will do it. Your conscience tells you to stop, and yet you can't because you do not have the power to break free from it. In all of these cases, try to understand that you have been possessed by evil spirits forcefully against your will while you were a baby or out of ignorance; they found their way into your body and life without your permission, but you do not even have the power to drive them away. This is where the blood of Jesus Christ comes into play.

Yes, you can be delivered and healed by the blood of Jesus Christ very simply. Christ blood is readily available for your use, but you have to play your own part too. Your role or part is to simply genuinely surrender your entire life totally to Christ, and the rest will be testimonies all through your life time. Most young Christians today, do not genuinely give their lives to Christ; this is where the whole problem lies. If you really do give your life to Christ, with little prayer efforts coupled with strict disciplined life, your life will be fully restored, no matter what the challenge had been. Every sin, evil, including curses or covenants hanging upon your life will be broken.

Prayer is a gift to you, and a great privilege. This gift is generally offered to all, and it is expected that everyone should become wielders of the great power which emanates from prayers. Nonetheless, these genuine facts remain that the average believer does not exercise the great power that is buried inside prayer. Many people do not want to pray: But you will do very well if you learn "THE ART OF WARFARE PRAYERS." Truly, the present temperature of a typical Christian's prayer life needs to rise up if they expect important breakthroughs in their lives. We shall be raising some serious prayer points here in this book for imminent salvation, healings, deliverance, empowerment, and breakthroughs.

For your information, there is a particular demon or group of demons that pull Christians away from praying; they project against brethren each time they want to pray, by making them feel weak, tired, and sleepy; and you would want to post-pone the prayers. Now, when you notice such, then comport yourself and strive in prayer. Shall we pray thus?

1. Every evil covenant, pulling me away from prayers, is destroyed by the blood of Jesus Christ.

2. Every evil covenant, binding me with water spirits, break by the blood of Jesus Christ.

3. Every evil association unknown to me, with marine spirits, cut off by the blood of Jesus Christ.

4. Every evil dedication made on my behalf by my parents to any demonic altar, be neutralized by the blood of Jesus Christ.

5. With the blood of Jesus Christ, I renounce every satanic crown and properties in my possession, in Jesus mighty name, amen.

By the time you finished praying the prayer points in this book; God would have completely re-established your true identity with Christ Jesus. Though this is my desire and expectation of you, much striving is also needed, and as well, full compliance to the instructions lay out by the writer.

GOD BLESS YOU RICHLY, IN JESUS NAME, AMEN.

CHAPTER ONE: EXCHANGE CHRIST BLOOD FOR

SINS, CURSES, COVENANTS, SICKNESSES, POVERTY, SPELLS, ENCHANTMENTS, DIVINATIONS, BONDAGE, POISON, BARRENNESS, UNFRUITFULNESS.

- ✓ THE SIMPLE PROCESS OF GENUINE REPENTANCE.
- ✓ THE SIMPLE PRAYER OF GENUINE REPENTANCE.
- ✓ THE POWERFUL PRAYERS TO ENFORCE THE POWER IN CHRIST BLOOD.

INTRODUCTION.

The Bible tells a pathetic story about a woman with the issue of blood for twelve years; and during this period of twelve of years, she continually bled without seizing. She heard about Jesus Christ who could heal her if only she could touch His garment. So, she managed and did touch the edge of His garment, and instantly she was healed.

Now, this is not only a miracle, it's indeed a mystery; but then, what actually happened? What is the source of power that healed this woman; is it the name of Jesus, or actually the garment she touched, or something else? We must not jump to conclude that it's the power in the name of Jesus or the garment; and what about the blood of Jesus? Now, let's get this simple understanding. The blood is the life and power behind any spiritual operation; and Christ blood has been confirmed to be the most potent, efficacious, and powerful weapon for any spiritual exchange to redeem (payment currency) man from the even the worst satanic or demonic bondage.

When we retrace our steps to examine the mystery of the Christ blood covenant of God's kingdom whose secret guarantees the mastery over life situations and circumstances, we have this simple reason and explanations to offer: Christ blood is the most powerful blood because it is God's blood; since Christ is the incarnation of God, it means Christ is God almighty who came to this earth in a human form, in the body of Jesus Christ. So Christ blood is directly

God's blood. Anything Christ blood touches (even inside Satan's domain), anywhere and anytime, it does the miraculous instantly.

The Bible makes us know that the divine secrets which are hidden in the scripture as simple verses are actually mysteries, for instance, when we are inquisitive to know these divine secrets, we come out as best in all areas of life. From the Bible perspective we understand mysteries to be of great value and strength in the kingdom to the children of God. So anytime one discovers in the Bible a mystery and you put it into practice, definitely, you shall testify of your successes, and each time you testify it becomes a natural to live. Take note, the secrets of the kingdom are placed in the hands of the prophets and apostles, and those who listen to them are blessed by such revelations (mysteries); because the great benefits which are buried inside mysteries must be firstly welcomed with open hands, and faith must be applied through practical work if you must enjoy it maximally.

THE MYSTERY OF THE BLOOD COVENANT.

The first mystery of the Christ blood covenant is, about 500 years before Christ came to this earth, a prophet of God saw in a vision and prophesied accordingly concerning the lord Jesus Christ, that His blood shall bring ALL-round salvation to mankind and everyone imprisoned by Satan in any way. Prophet Zechariah wrote, "Rejoice greatly, O daughter of Zion; shout, O daughter of Jerusalem: behold, the king cometh unto thee: he is just, and having salvation;

lowly, and riding upon an ass, and upon a colt the foal of an ass. As for thee also, by the blood of thy covenant I have sent forth thy prisoners out of the pit wherein is no water. Turn you to the stronghold, ye prisoners of hope: even today do I declare that I will render double unto thee."- Zechariah 9:9, 11-12. KJV.

"...thy king cometh...", as indicated above signify Jesus Christ, and "by the blood of thy covenant I have sent forth thy prisoners out ...", indicated that the blood of Jesus Christ is the blood of the covenant between Christ and all of humanity, which redeem all of us from every curse, covenant, sickness, disease, poverty, bondage, etc., and by His grace releases upon us all manner of blessings.

ENGAGEMENTS WITH CHRIST BLOOD COVENANT.

The engagement of the mystery of Christ blood covenant is very important and they include:

- **WARFARE PRAYERS:** Involving pleading the blood of Jesus Christ and/or call-up the miraculous power in the blood of Christ to enable victorious winnings.
- **COMMUNION TABLES:** When we eat the communion bread and drink the wine, as symbols of Christ flesh and blood, by faith, we stamp out sicknesses, diseases, poison, ailments, weaknesses, bondages, etc., and our strength are renewed.
- **BLOOD SPRINKLING:** Being Christ the Passover lamb, the sprinkling of Christ blood can serve the same purpose as the

symbol or representative of the blood sprinkled on the doors-posts of Israelites in Egypt against deaths, sicknesses, diseases, evil projections, etc., which automatically pass over their households, and even forty years afterwards in the wilderness.

EXCHANGE CHRIST BLOOD FOR EVERYTHING.

A HEAP OF BLOOD.

A preacher once told us a story about how the blood of Christ saves and protects from all manner of projected evil activities against the genuine children of God who live under the coverage of the blood covenant. It is about a lady who lives alone in a neighborhood. She was the out-going evangelical type who had many female and male friends; but among this retinue of friends, there were jealous few who hated her kind of lifestyle. At a point in time, her haters plotted to eliminate her so as to put an end to her life, and let's see what becomes of her Christianity where she kept bragging about her savior, Jesus Christ.

On a particular night, at about 03:00hrs in the early morning , her assailant went to her apartment to carry out the assignment, but on getting to there, lo and behold, he saw a heap of blood in the main room, he was stunned and confused so he quickly left the scene. As he hurried away, he noticed someone saw him but he didn't look back. In the morning, the lady was still sleeping because she did a night vigil, but the supposed assailant, out of a guilty conscience, came to look and probably confirm what he saw in the night whether it was true or not.

As he approached the gate of the lady's apartment he saw two men walking towards him, and suddenly he began to scream, "I was not the person who killed her; I saw blood everywhere when I got here and I turned back immediately. Someone else must have killed before I got there; I swear I didn't kill her." The two men were baffled because they couldn't understand what he was referring to; so they asked him, what are you saying? And so, he narrated what transpired, how they plotted to kill the lady, and how he went to carry out the evil assignment, only to be confronted with a heap of blood in the front room.

The three of them turned and looked toward the direction of the lady's apartment, but everything looked intact, and as they were wondering over the whole issue, the lady came out of her apartment and greeted the three of them with a broad smile on her face. So, the man made a confession to the lady; she was surprised although she believed God protect His people every time. She gave glory to God almighty for the lesson they all learned: God cover us with a protective covering from our common enemy and his cohorts.

A PROTECTIVE HEDGE.

Also, it was told about a group of Arabian Christian merchants in the olden days, which embarked on a distant journey between two commercial cities. At night, they stopped in the opened desert to rest for the night. Before they slept in the open space, they prayed in the name of Jesus Christ and then slept; but unknown to them, there was a group of desert robbers that have been lurking around with intent to rob them while they sleep at night.

During the first night, as they were sleeping the robbers struck and attempted to step in between them as they lay on the ground, but they could not ; each attempt to step into their midst was met with invincible brink wall. They see them though, but each time the robbers tried to stretch their hands to pick their bags, they discovered there exists a glass wall which makes it difficult for them (robbers) to penetrate. The same thing happened the second night, and they (robbers) were perturbed and frustrated. Meanwhile, the Christian brethren never knew what was going on.

In the morning of the third day, just as they were preparing to begin the last lap of their journey, these robbers came and greeted them; they confessed to the brethren what they have been trying to do to them but failed. They went further to ask what was protecting them from being harmed by them this past three days. They said all attempts to rob them for two consecutive nights were unsuccessful. The brethren were not surprised at all, because they knew Christ protection was real due to the knowledge of the secret of the blood covenant. The brethren answered and said,"It is Christ Jesus that protects them, and shall continue to protect them at all times." The robbers on realizing this truth went quickly on their knees and gave their lives to Christ.

A CHRISTIAN CONVERTED TO ISLAM, BUT THEN HAD A SUPERNATURAL ENCOUNTER WITH JESUS IN A DREAM.

Mike Westerfield was in crisis mode. Raised as a "religious Christian," Mike was involved in his church and even preached on occasion. But when he had no answers for the Muslim inmates who were giving him Islamic literature at a Florida prison, he did the unthinkable. He converted to Islam.

Mike just wasn't sure about the Trinity or how to defend it, and the Muslim prisoners whom he visited each day sensed a weakness.

I ended up abandoning Christianity and embraced Islam. I was a Muslim for 12 years and attended an Islamic University for some time in hopes of becoming a Muslim imam or scholar. After about 7 years of being a faithful Muslim, I started rethinking Jesus' role after learning more about Islam, its deception, and lies."

"I started looking back into my old books on Christian apologetics from a Bible college I attended and began reading the Bible. I also started reviewing Lee Strobel's literature in the Case for Christ, Case for Faith, and watched Ravi Zacharias' videos.

I was eventually introduced to Abdu Murray who was with Embrace the Truth International; he was an Ex-Muslim turned Christian apologist.

He was the first Ex-Muslim I met and could share my thoughts and doubts with. He talked openly with me and did not condemn me. He listened as to why I was now considering leaving Islam after being fanatical about it at one time.”

“In 2012, I ended up having a dream about Jesus and in it I was covered in his blood! I couldn't understand why I had this dream but it was truly amazing and I couldn't get it out of my mind. Jesus' blood filled the scene in my dream. I tried to run from it, but it covered me entirely! I felt such peace and love, and Jesus' dark brown eyes pierced my soul!”

“I called Abdu Murray and told him about my dream, and he was shocked! The night I had the dream, he and Josh McDowell had prayed that Jesus would appear to me in a dream and show himself to me!”

“The God of Heaven graciously heard their prayer and sent a dream that convinced me His blood was more than sufficient to forgive me of my sins. Hallelujah!”

"Right then, I knew in my heart that Jesus was the Son of God. But leaving Islam was not easy."

"Finally, I fully surrendered everything to Jesus a year later in January of 2013 and was born again! It was glorious! Jesus never gave up on me."

"Today, I am blessed to have completed a master's degree in Christian studies. How privileged I am to serve Jesus Christ as my Lord and Savior. I truly love sharing the gospel and especially with Muslims who are in desperate need of the forgiveness that only the Cross of Christ can bring."

Whether it is healings, protection, deliverance, etc, the blood of Christ Jesus in the covenant does the EXCHANGES. All you need to do is to enter into the covenant with the blood of Christ and every other thing will fall into their normal places. Once you genuinely give up on living in sin (I mean living a sin-free life), not a hypocritical life, and fully surrender your life to Christ. This is as simple as it can be; you have just received divine protection through the covenant with blood.

THE SIMPLE PEOCESS OF GENUINE REPENTANCE.

If you really want to benefit from this book, you would have to totally surrender your life to the lordship of Jesus Christ absolutely, devoid of any hypocrisy or pretence. Genuine repentance is required from anyone who wishes to enjoy the blood covenant relationship with Christ Jesus. The secret in the blood of the covenant is that, it is actually the blood of God almighty who came down from heaven to us in the person of Jesus Christ by reason of the incarnation. This blood is not the blood of chicken, goat, lamb, sheep, pig, cow, dog, camel, horse, monkey, chimpanzee, gorilla, or ordinary human blood; it is the blood of GOD.

The simple process of renunciation of sins entails conviction, confession, repentance, and forsaking of the sins. If you claim to have given your life to Christ but you are still struggling with, or committing sins, these special prayers points will work for you; but if you are struggling with sins because of the nature of your work, or the environment where you live, or the relationships you are keeping, or your present financial condition, or even the church you attend presently, etc.; but you can try and adjust by effecting some changes. Yes, you can change your job; your accommodation, your friends, and even the church you attend. Don't get hooked up to your parents, friends, employer, fiancé or fiancée, because of financial assistance you get from them. Pray fervently and move on.

A genuine child of God does not need a physical supervision since he or she has the Holy Spirit and the church. If you truly are able to establish a transparent relationship with Christ as spelt out above, you will begin to experience inherent power in the blood of Christ on daily basis. You will be set free from all powers of darkness as you dedicate your time to pray the suggested prayer points in this book. I do have my own personal experiences and testimonies, so also, other genuine Christians do have theirs as well.

THE PRAYER OF GENUINE REPENTANCE

My father in heaven, I come to you this moment with a serious conviction that I do need you now. I can no longer help myself to come out of the grasp of Satan, but I do believe that your son Jesus Christ can help get me out of his clutches; therefore, I surrender my entire life to Him today. Lord Jesus, forgive me of my past sinful life: I committed very many atrocious sins, including fornications, adultery, idolatry, homosexuals, materialism, drug addictions, drunkenness, robberies, (name them), etc. I repent of them all now; from today, I give them all up; I shall not go back to any of them again. So lord, give me power to live a life of righteousness for you, in Jesus name I pray, amen.

THE PRAYER TO ENFORCE THE POWER IN CHRIST BLOOD.

PRAYER POINTS.

- Every serpentine spirit caging my destiny, be thou consumed by the blood of Christ.
- Every serpentine spirit in my blood stream, be thou neutralized by the blood of Christ.
- Let the power in the blood of Christ redeem my destiny in Christ mighty name.
- I command all my stolen virtues to return to me now, Christ Jesus name.

- My father in heaven, bring forth my personal revival as the blood of Christ releases me from the pangs of demons, in Jesus name.
- By the blood of Christ, I prophesy that I will to my promised inheritance, in the powerful name of Christ.
- Whichever that says I shall not move forward, I plead the blood of Christ for its arrest in the mighty name of Jesus
- My father, my father, if I have fallen behind in any area of my life, I plead the blood of Chris Jesus to empower me to recover all lost opportunities, in Jesus name.
- Blood of Christ Jesus, blood of Christ Jesus, redeem me now from all powers of darkness, in the mighty name of Jesus.
- Blood of Christ Jesus, blood of Christ Jesus, flush out every evil deposit in my spiritual system, in Jesus precious name.

CHAPTER TWO: HIDE YOURSELF IN CHRIST BLOOD

For Salvation, Protection, & Deliverance.

"In whom we have redemption through his blood, the forgiveness of sins, according to the riches of his grace." - **Ephesians 1:7.**

"And grieve not the Holy Spirit of God, whereby ye are sealed unto the day of redemption." - **Ephesians 4:30.**

"And the blood shall be to you for a token upon the houses where ye are: and when I see the blood, I will Passover you, and the plague shall not be upon you to destroy you, when I smite the land of Egypt." - **Exodus 12:13.**

The word "redemption" has a fuller meaning than "saving" or "deliverance." It means "deliverance with a price." This costly price was paid by Jesus Christ; and the currency used to purchase it was Christ blood. This currency (Christ blood) exchange, covers a complete range of all human need, including forgiveness, salvation, deliverance, protection, peace, love, reconciliation, security, victory, knowledge, wisdom, healing, fellowship, and authority over Satan and his cohorts. The power in the blood of Jesus Christ provides all of the above for us to live of daily victory.

THE BLOOD OF CHRIST REDEEMED (SAVED) US.

Christians all over the world have knowledge of the blood of Jesus; it's commonly sung in church hymns, and easily comes to mind during communion services. Apart from that, very many Christians do not deeply understand the inherent power in the blood and what it provides for us every time. Now, because of this ignorance many couldn't use it to ward-off many activities of the devil on daily basis. Remember, blood was presented throughout the entire Bible, from Genesis to Revelation. Every major event in the Bible was done through blood sacrifices. This is to demonstrate the very important role blood has to play; check out notable sacrifices carried out in the Old Testament, such as Abel Noah, Abraham, Isaac, Passover, Moses; none was done without blood being used.

Blood was of paramount importance to God that was why He accepted animal sacrifices to cover their sins: But for the sins of the whole world, a more potent, precious, and powerful blood was needed, so, the blood of Christ Jesus, whom God loved so dearly was used to redeem mankind from perishing. The scripture says, "We have redemption through His blood." You are aware the Bible tells us that Satan deceived Adam and collected the authority (power) over the earth from him, and since then death came and the earth and all things in it were cursed; and Satan became the master of the universe. In other to collect back the authority from Satan, God developed a redemption plan, which needed a greater magnitude of blood sacrifice, and the blood of the beloved son of God was required. This is the greatest achievement the blood of Christ Jesus has accomplished. The blood sacrifice of Christ Jesus set you free from every curse, covenant, or entanglement with Satan and his cohorts.

THE BLOOD OF CHRIST AVAIL US OF FELLOWSHIP WITH GOD.

After God made Adam, he was alone for quite a while before God brought Eve to Adam to become his companion, but meanwhile Adam had fellowship with God because he was God's friend. After Eve joined Adam, the communion with God continued until Serpent came and deceived and swindled them of the authority over the earth. As this occurred, the communion fellowship with God stopped: But it has to be restored, and it was restored through the blood of Christ Jesus. Today, every bona-fide child of God enjoys a communion fellowship, which only the blood of Christ made available

The scripture says, "Having boldness to enter the holiest by the blood of Jesus." Fellowship with God means an intimate relationship between God and man. When Satan snatched the authority from Adam, sin then separated man from God until God through Jesus Christ came to restore it. The blood of Christ is very powerful, it enables you to boldly enter into the presence of God with confidence and courage to ask for whatever you might need and it shall be granted unto you. The door of communion between man and God which was shut has now been opened wide for us to go through; by communion, it means something deeper than mere religious rituals.

THE BLOOD OF CHRIST JESUS PROTECTS US.

The Biblical story of pharaoh tell us about the stubborn king of Egypt who refused to let the children of Israel go away from the land of Egypt, and God said, He was going judge the king and the people of Egypt. On the night, just before they embark on the journey out of Egypt, God instructed the Israelites to kill a lamb each household, and apply the blood on the door-post; and that when He sees the blood, He will Passover them. At mid-night god sent an angel of death over the entire land of Egypt, to kill every first-born of both humans and animals, and it was so.

The scripture says, "When I see the blood, I will pass over you." The blood as indicated in this scripture is a symbol of the blood of Christ, which if applied, can protect us and stop death, sicknesses, diseases, poverty, etc., from coming to us. Each time or whenever we apply the blood of Christ to the very door-post of our lives by faith, we will experience a powerful force that will appear to bring down every demonic power behind curses, covenants, poverty, sicknesses, bondages that tries to enter into your body. The blood of Christ Jesus is infinite, unfailing, and unlimited in supply.

THE BLOOD OF CHRIST JESUS HEALS US.

I have been participating in the Lord's Supper in my local church for a very long time now and each time I do, my mind goes straight to divine healings of my body, and that's how it has been these past twenty-five years. During the time of the communion services, we pray to God to deliver us from besetting sins, which are usually the cause of sicknesses to our bodies. The full power of the blood weighs against sins, sicknesses, diseases, ailments, depression, etc., and each time we participate in Holy Communion services, the blood of Christ exercises its power and authority against every form of weaknesses in the body.

The scripture says, "By his stripes we are healed." Every day, we need healings to our bodies, and the blood of Christ is freely available to do it for us all. You can ask for as much as you want because there is no overdose nor does it have any detrimental side effects. The healings are made available through the ever flowing blood of Christ Jesus.

THE BLOOD OF CHRIST GIVES US AUTHORITY (POWER) OVER SATAN.

The devil in most of his activities try to confuse us so that we do not know how important the power in the blood of Christ is, because the day you get to know it, you will no longer be afraid of him anymore. So, know this day that the blood of Christ Jesus gives you power above Satan and his cohorts. This is what the scripture says, "And they overcame him by the blood of the lamb, and by the word of their testimony." If you believe this scripture you have just read, and then know for sure you have defeated him; now make your ways right with Christ by genuinely confessing your sins to Him, renouncing them and inviting Christ into your heart. There is enormous power in the blood of Christ which was shed for you; we must continually plead and declare it over every area of our lives.

HIDE IN CHRIST BLOOD AND BE SAVED.

The lord Jesus Christ is keener to save, and able to actually save from any and every human affliction. Very many Christians do not even understand what Christ really saves us from. So, what and who then can Christ save us from? Here are few of them:

SAVE FROM WORLDILINESS

We are saved and delivered spiritually from this present evil world. As we accept Christ as personal lord and savior, God releases the Holy Spirit to us, thereby translating un into God's kingdom.

SAVED FROM THE DEVIL AND HIS COHORTS.

Satan holds sinners captive through the love of the world. The Bible says, "For this purpose the son of man was revealed, that He might undo the works of the devil." Another scripture says, "Jesus died to bring to nothing the devil who had power over death."

SAVED FROM DEATH

The scripture says, "We are dead in our trespasses and sins." We are walking corpses, yes, we are living but dead. We discovered through Christ that what we termed as death is actually sleep. Christ says, "I am the resurrection and the life! he who believes in me, though he dies, yet he shall live."

SAVED FROM FAKE LIFE.

Christ says, "I have come so that they might have life, and that they might have it more abundantly." This goes a long way to show that the life non-Christians are living is fake life. Christ Jesus has come to give us the real and original life; but to obtain it, He says, "..You must be born again..."

SAVED FROM OURSELVES.

Truly speaking, we are the worst enemies of ourselves. We lack self-control; this is the worst enemy of man, a man without self-control. The Bible says, "A man's worst enemies will be right in his own home." Yes, most times we sin against our own souls, for instance, lying, evil thoughts, fornication, adultery, etc. Remember what the lord Jesus Christ said, "If your eye causes you to sin, pluck it out; if your hand causes you to sin, cut it off." When a man lives without sin, devil will not be able to impede his progress, harm him, frustrate him, or put him in bondage.

SAVED FROM SIN.

The greatest and most important thing Christ saved us from is sin. The scripture says, "She shall bear a son, and you shall call his name Jesus: for he shall save his people from their sins." Once a man is saved from this evil called sin, he is ninety percent free from life's major problem. Where there is no sin, Satan or devil cannot come around you; also when sin is not present, the attacks from Satan and his cohorts become non-existent to a considerable level. So, sin attracts most of the problems that confronts us in life. Thanks to Christ for delivering us from the power of sin.

SAVED TO THE MAXIMUM.

There is no limitation to the salvation that Jesus Christ provided through His redemptive work for mankind. Christ redemptive work is total and complete which covers every area of man's endeavors. The scripture says, "He is able also to save to the uttermost those who draw near to God through Him." He is able to deliver and save from all known human affliction.

ALL PURPOSE PRAYERS

APPLYING THE BLOOD OF CHRIST.

I have rendered here an ALL-PURPOSE PRAYER POINTS meant to address from the root all manner of human affliction. It should be noted that these Holy Spirit vomited prayer points are prepared for Christians who are born-again; but if you are not sure whether or not you are born-again, then go back to chapter one, and formally give your life to Christ before you start the prayers.

The secret of the mystery of the Christ blood covenant cannot be over-emphasized; but if you pray with faith these prayer points, there is no doubt you would give testimonies instantly because the Holy Spirit is fully involved.

A FACT FORMULA.

JESUS CHRIST = JESUS BLOOD = JESUS CHRIST.

The name of 'Jesus Christ' is equal to the name 'Jesus Blood' and vice versa; the name Christ and the Blood are exactly the same. The life of Christ is in the blood of Christ, so, there would not have been Jesus Christ without Jesus Blood. When God the father sent Jesus Christ to come to the earth to redeem it, it was His blood that was of uppermost importance and significance Him. This is why the emphasis is on the blood.

Remember, five hundred years before Christ actually came to earth to redeem it from the hands of Satan and hand it to over to us, it was prophesied (Leveticus17:11), that the savoir would come to shed His blood to redeem man. Secondly, the importance of the blood is seen in scripture, "For the life of the flesh is in the blood: and I have given it to you upon the altar to make

atonement for your soul."

PRAYER POINTS.

Read these scriptures: Galatians 3:13 – 14; 2Timothy 4:18; Colosians1:13, 2:15.

- Thank God for His mighty power to save to the uttermost and for the power to deliver from any form of bondage, in the name Christ.

- Every gate opened to the enemy by my foundation, be closed forever with the blood of Christ.
- The power inherent in the blood of Christ, take me away from the sins of my ancestral lineage, in the name of Christ Jesus.
- Blood of Jesus, blood of Jesus, take away any label of lack of progress out of every area of my destiny, in Jesus name.
- Blood of Jesus, blood of Jesus, release the fire of the Holy Spirit, to wash and purify all the organs in my body, in the mighty of Jesus.
- Blood of Jesus, blood of Jesus, be thou transfused to every blood vessel in my body, Christ name.
- Blood of Jesus, blood of Jesus, wash my system thoroughly and flush down every deposit of satanic inheritance, in the name of Christ.
- Blood of Jesus, blood of Jesus, destroy every trace of ancestral, guardian, and familiar spirits in my life, in the name of Christ Jesus.
- Blood of Jesus, blood of Jesus, loose the hold of any ancestral bloodshed of animals and/or human beings affecting my life, in Jesus mighty name.
- Blood of Jesus, blood of Jesus, flush out every garment of ancestral infirmity, disease, sickness, untimely death, poverty, disfavor, dishonor, shame, failure at the edge of miracles, which has passed down to my generation, in the mighty name of Christ Jesus.

These prayer points truly addressed the root cause of your affliction, so, there may be need to repeat them every week until you begin to see tangible results.

GOD BLESS YOU.

CHAPTER THREE: SOAK YOURSELF IN CHRIST BLOOD FOR

Salvation, Healings, deliverance.

- ✓ Introduction.
- ✓ Washing Dirty Clothes Scenario.
- ✓ Biblical Quotes That Support Soaking.
- ✓ How To Soak Body In Christ Blood.
- ✓ Declaration.
- ✓ Powerful Prayer Points.

INTRODUCTION

Ordinarily, to soak means to lie down and remain motionless for a stipulated in a volume of liquid in a container or large mass of liquid usually water. It simply means lying completely inside a liquid content or pool of liquid; but for the purpose of this book, the Biblical concept connotes when a person lies down on the bed or on the ground motionless and not talking to anyone. We soak ourselves with to find out something from our hearts or minds; it involves how to calm the mind as we stay in the presence of God. It disciplines the ever busy body and causes it to patiently wait for God to connect with him while we tarry. As we soak ourselves in God, we give permission to His word and His Spirit to thoroughly wash-up every dirt and stains (sins) in our lives. This is sometimes called 'quiet time'.

The main purpose of soaking is to connect to God from our hearts. If one really wants to connect to God, he or she must follow due diligence to observe the rules such as, being alone, being alert, being free from all distractions, ready to connect, and available to receive from God. When you proceed without making sure everything is well articulated, you may not be able to truly connect with God, and the resultant consequences is guilt. The simple reason is, we are not prepared, and secondly we go to God with long prayer requests, petitions, supplications, etc. Soaking, which is likened to quiet time is actually a time to be quiet so that we can hear from God. It's a time to present to God those challenges in our lives; you are aware God knows everything about you. At this time you do not need to tell Him what your problems are, but rather just be quiet and listen to what He may speak or do to you.

When you lie down and just keep quiet before Him, it shows your humility and at the same time slows you down, thereby pulling you into worship. When you soak yourself in the blood, you shut your lips but open your heart to God. Take note here, the word 'soak' as used, is not a biblical terminology, but it has been applied to drive home the point I am making; when you enter into His presence and soak yourself in the blood with all humility, and without speaking a word, the life in the blood of Christ will deal with every situations or conditions that brought you to Him.

The practical approach to soaking oneself in the blood of Christ Jesus is to establish or choose a particular place and time of meeting; know the exact time and avoid distractions, start with worship song or worship music playing in the background. It is necessary to having writing materials by your side because revelations might come. Practice this regularly and very soon your wavy thoughts would come under the control of the Holy Spirit, healings, deliverances, salvation, Holy Spirit empowerment such as the power gifts, vocal gifts, etc. will begin to manifest. When you continually soak yourself in the Christ covenant blood, you will not only be saved, healed, and delivered from all manner of evil machinations, you will be empowered with the power gifts and the vocal gifts to enable you to serve the almighty God.

WASHING DIRTY CLOTHES SCENARIO.

Every chemical agent that cleans surfaces of clothes, beddings, vessels, plates, etc., are called compounds and are applied to remove dirt, dist, stains, bad odors, including substances which spoils surfaces. The cleaning agents are chemicals that are applied so as to minimize tensions on the surface of the commodity, and allow water to wash it properly. The two common agents for cleaning are soaps and detergents

A detergent is a synthetic chemical which cleans very well and is applied as an active agent on surfaces with soft and/or hard water. Most dirt is naturally oily and insoluble inside water. The oily dirt is removed by a particular chemical in the soap called micelle during the washing process. The soap's micelle is a very powerful stain and dirt remover; as long as the dirt has oily nature, the soap's micelle must remove it.

SIMILARITIES BETWEEN CHRIST BLOOD AND DETERGENTS

When we soak are clothes for washing , the purpose is to remove every dirt, dust, stains, bad odors, and other unwanted deposits on the surfaces of our clothes, plates, vessels, etc.; the idea is to bring back the original condition of that commodity. The same thing applies to blood generally; the blood of chickens, goats, rams, etc. could be used to remove some sicknesses, diseases, infertility, bad luck; while human blood , to a considerable extent could be used to exchange (reverse) for many evil projections against an individual, but the eventual resultant consequences are unpalatable. Now, the blood of Christ Jesus is the only blood that can exchange or reverse every evil affliction against any human. Immediately the blood of Christ is applied by any human who has established a covenant relationship with Christ, will automatically receive exchange from sickness to health (healing), from bondage to freedom (deliverance), from sinning to righteousness (salvation), from spiritual poverty to spiritual riches, etc.

BIBLICAL QUOTES THAT SUPPORTS SOAKING.

SOAK YOURSELF IN CHRIST BLOOD.

Before you step out each day, make sure you pray fervently and as well adequately soak yourself in Christ blood. Gift of life is the greatest gift from God; if you sleep and didn't wake up the next morning, everything about your life has come to an end. It is therefore very imperative to give thanks to the almighty God. Jesus Christ knew all of the time that Satan was after Him, to destroy Him. So, He prayed always to put asunder all the evil works of Satan against Him. Satan is also after your life too, so be ware.

We are always at war against Satan, and as you may know, the weapons of our warfare are not carnal but mighty through God…, therefore we are duty bound to recognize the importance of Christ blood as the mightier weapon we need to fight the common enemy. The scripture expressly tells us that the enemy was defeated by the aid of Christ blood. "And they overcame him by the blood of the lamb," – Revelation 12:11. KJV. This is the reason why you must soak yourself in the blood of Jesus Christ always because that is where all the protection you needed to overcome Satan is kept.

Each time the enemy (Satan) confronts you, quickly show him the blood of Christ; it is the ID (Identification Card) you must wave at him any time you come to his roadblock on your way. "And they overcame him by the blood of the lamb...", actually means, pleading the blood of Christ at point the devil confronts you. Now, I am encouraging you to always soak yourself in Christ blood; the meaning is this, you may not need your ID when you are in your full regalia (uniform) because soaking yourself in the blood is likened to someone who wears the full army camouflage. Any roadblock mounted by security operatives, freely allows any fully dressed security personnel to pass because of the uniform; so also, in the spirit realm when you soaked yourself in the blood of Christ, the devil waves you to pass immediately without delay because Satan and his cohorts see the blood all over your body. Satan cannot withstand the blood of Christ Jesus, and also, he cannot withstand the sound of the name of Jesus Christ when it is pronounced. Those who fully soaked themselves in the blood of Christ Jesus always carry greater grace that causes Satan to be afraid.

CHRIST BLOOD; DIVINE BATH

Endeavor to soak yourself in the Blood of Christ; it is the Divine Bath for the Soul. While the world still wallow in ignorance of animals and human sacrifices, in contrast, Christians with exuding confidence look back to a perfect once and final sacrifice of Christ blood as atonement for our sins of the past, the present and even in the future. When we take a view of the work of Christ on that faithful Good Friday and we quickly remembered what it stood for, we recognized that our perfect priest offered a perfect sacrifice perfectly because he is holy and so, the infinite value of his atonement can save everybody from every human affliction. Read Hebrews chapters 7, 8, 9.

Now, this is how to soak body in the blood of Christ Jesus. I repeat again, it is the blood of Christ that is a divine bath for the soul. As you dip your body into the unlimited, ever- flowing river of His blood, He takes our sin, like a flashing torch light and drops it in the ocean of his love where it is dissolved.

HOW TO SOAK YOUR BODY IN CHRIST BLOOD.

*As you plead the blood...in prayer.. **Ex 12:13***

*As you respond to Christ call...to serve. Joshua 22:5; **Matthew 6:24***

*As you perpetuate (grow) your faith in Christ, to know Him more & more.. **Phi 3:10.***

*As you put your faith in action... to trust and believe Him.. **Psalm 37:40; 62:8.***

*As you cry genuinely for deliverance... **Obadiah 1:17.***

As you participate (partake) in communion services.... **Matthew 26:26-28**.

*As you attend regularly Bible studies....***Hebrews 10:25**.

*As you show genuine love out of a pure heart.....***Romans 8:35,38,39**.

*As you are determined to draw closer (Show interest) to God ...***Isaiah 1:18**.

As you develop a desire to partake in Christ sufferings ... **Philippians 3:10**.

*As you make effort daily to draw near unto God and live a holy and righteous life.... **James 4:8; Hebrews 10:38**.*

When your conscience besieges you do not run to find another scapegoat. Jesus is the scapegoat who alone has successfully carried our sins outside the camp.

He is the lamb whose blood taketh away all our sins; just go and soak yourself in the blood of Christ and you are made whole.

Take that sin, sickness, disease, curse, covenant, poverty, failure, frustration, emotions, trauma, bondage, pain, etc.; yes, take it to Christ blood bath and soak all of them in the blood.

Jesus is the propitiation who has gone into the holy place with his own blood to make atonement, to adorn the holy place with his sacred blood.

He is able to save completely (Heb. 7:25-26)! He 'put away sin by the sacrifice of himself' (Heb. 9:26).

POWERFUL PRAYER POINTS USING THE BLOOD OF CHRIST JESUS.

The Blood of Jesus is the mighty weapon we shall use for this warfare; by the time you complete these prayer points you would have learned and mastered how to pray, using the blood of Jesus as a weapon. Read 2 Corinthians 10:3-5.

YOUR DECLARATION:

> *"And they overcame him by the blood of the Lamb, and by the Word of their testimony; as a weapon." -* ***Revelation 12:11. KJV.***

In the mighty name of Christ Jesus, I am truly a born-again child of the most high God. I trust and have faith in God the father, as well as Christ Jesus His son, and the blessed Holy Spirit who fills me up from the inside. I fully trust and believe in the immovable powerful Word of God.

This is what I believe:

- ✓ That life and death are in power of my tongue.
- ✓ That this confession I make today with the power in my tongue, shall be into life.

✓ That I shall prosper according to the Words which the lord has this day put in my mouth.

As it is written "Whoso eateth my flesh, and drinketh my blood, hath eternal life; and I will raise him up at the last day. For my flesh is meat indeed, and my blood is drink indeed. He eateth my flesh, and drinketh my blood, dwelleth in me, and I in him." --John 6:54, 55. Lord, with firm faith in my mind I stretch forth my arm with this cup of your blood (Lamb of God) and I consume it, and I will possess eternal life.

Let the blood of Christ quicken every dead thing within me; and let the strength of my life be resurrected by the blood. Let the blood invigorate, revitalize, remold and revive every buried abilities and gifts of the Holy Spirit within me. Every inherited self-damaging demonic deposit in my body be flushed out. Let the blood of Christ purify my spiritual and physical blood circulating systems. Let the blood of Christ transform everything in my life to become anew.

My lord Jesus, please make me drunk with your blood and I shall be filled with eternal life. It is written, "Be strong in the Lord and in the power of His might." My father and my lord, I request that you become my very might and strength each day of my life. Father, do not allow me to fall into the traps of my enemies and the praise of your name will never depart from my mouth all the days of my life. With my heart I truly believe the Word of God in my heart and with my mouth I have made this confession unto salvation. Lord Jesus, performed unto me as I have prayed according to your word, in Christ Jesus wonderful and gracious name. Amen.

KEEP SILENT FOR 5-10 MINUTES.

(Listen to the Holy Spirit).

DO SOME PRAISE AND WORSHIP.

Father I bless your Holy name for the great rewards and availability of the blood of son Jesus Christ.

Therefore, I stand my ground because of the provision of Christ blood to declare overwhelming victory over sin, death, Satan, his agents, and the world.

- I pour out the covenant blood of Christ upon every unyielding challenge confronting my life.
- I plead the covenant blood of Christ Jesus upon my spirit, soul, body, and destiny.
- I soak my spirit, soul, body, and destiny in the covenant blood of Christ.
- With a firm grip I embrace the covenan blood of Christ Jesus as a defense against every power projections that will attempt to withstand me, in the name of Jesus.

- With the covenant blood of Christ I shut every door opened to the demons in ignorance, in the name of Christ Jesus.

- By the covenant blood of Jesus, I am redeemed from the hands of Satan and his cohorts, in the mighty name of Christ Jesus.

- By the covenant blood of Christ Jesus, I walk in newness of life, from all sins and sorrows, in the mighty name of Christ Jesus.

- I placed a permanent curse on every activities of darkness against my life, by the covenant blood of Christ Jesus.

- Any dark power delegated against me, receive the blood of Christ and be dissolved, in the mighty name of Jesus.

- I up-root from the roots every work of darkness in my life and dissolve in the blood of Christ Jesus.

- I paralyze and erase by the blood of Christ Jesus every spirit of demotion and stagnation, in the name of Jesus.

CHAPTER FOUR: EAT CHRIST FLESH AND DRINK CHRIST BLOOD FOR

(Healings, Deliverances and Eternal Life).

- ✓ Introduction.
- ✓ Similarity: Christ Flesh & Blood And Medication.
- ✓ Biblical Quotes Which Supports Eating Christ Flesh.
- ✓ Declaration.
- ✓ Powerful Prayer Points.

INTRODUCTION.

Jesus Christ says, "I am that bread of life. Your fathers did eat manna in the wilderness, and are dead. This is the bread which cometh down from heaven, that a man may eat thereof, and not die. I am the living bread which came down from heaven: if any eat of this bread, he shall live forever: and the bread that I will give is my flesh, which I will give for the life of the world. The Jews therefore strove amongst themselves, saying, how can this man give us His flesh to eat? Then Jesus said unto them, verily, verily, I say unto you, except ye eat the flesh of the son of man, and drink his blood, ye have no life in you. Whoso eateth my flesh, and drinketh, hath eternal life; and I will raise him up at the last day. For my flesh is meat indeed, and my blood is drink indeed. He that eateth my flesh and drinketh my blood dwelleth in me, and I in him. As the living father hath sent me, and I live by the father: so he that eatetn me, even he shall live by me. This is that bread which came down from heaven: not as your fathers did eat manna, and are dead: he that eateth of this bread shall live forever."

As he admonishes the Corinthian church, Paul said," Wherefore whosoever shall eat this bread and drink this cup unworthily shall be guilty of the body and the blood of the lord. But let a man examine himself, and so let him eat of that bread, and drink of that cup. For he that eateth and drinketh unworthily, eateth and drinketh damnation to himself, not discerning the body of the lord. For this cause many are weak and sickly among you, and many sleep,"

Conversely, we are being informed that when you eat worthily, it is filled with healing and nourishing ingredients and power. So, if you are the type that religiously partakes of the Lord's Table you will not become weak, sickly, or even die premature death; and you may not need medication from the doctors and nurses, knowing full well you possess a divine nature. If you believe this simple scriptural statement, and backed it up with your faith in Christ Jesus: it does work. The purpose of this book is to pull you out of the ignorance of not knowing the great importance of the lord 'supper; and to re-establish you so that you can continue or in case you have not been participating as some people do, you can come back to your senses. It is a great privilege to partake of the lord's supper always because in it are healings, health nourishments, divine health, life, and eternal life.

SIMILARITY: CHRIST FLESH & BLOOD AND MEDICATION.

When someone become weak and sick, he or she goes to the pharmacy or drug store to get some medicines, but in severe cases there might be need to consult the physician. The doctor checks your body to find out what the problem is, and appropriate medicines will be recommended to be taken. People are sick everywhere, including professing Christians, WHY?

Genuine born-again spirit-filled Christians, who truly understand their divine nature and position in Christ; who faithfully partake in the Lord's Table, can hardly be sick to need the doctor's attention. Yes, minor inconveniencing sickness could occur most probably because of the condition of the environment or weather, which may result to flu, colds, or feverish conditions, etc: But real body weakness or sickness which puts one down wouldn't come to the typical Christian who faithfully partakes in the Lord's Supper.

When one regularly participates in communion services, it is likened to someone who goes to the drug store weekly to pick up health supplements to aid the proper function of the body immune system to forestall a future breakdown. So, the weekly or monthly communion services are similar to medication. Surely, the flesh and the blood of Christ Jesus which is represented on the communion table as bread and wine actually works efficaciously. On the Lord's Table, physical sicknesses resulting from natural conditions, or sicknesses induced by demons can be healed; you can as well be delivered from other demonic afflictions caused by evil projections as you regularly participate.

What qualifies one to participate in Holy Communion services is as simple as you can imagine. The first prerequisite is that you are born-again; next to that is, try as much as possible to live the 'righteous life', free yourself from all known besetting sins, and have faith in Christ. Many Christian communicants do not go to hospitals, clinics, or health centers from year to year because of the sustaining power in the bread and wine they often take during Holy Communion Services which represent the flesh and the blood of Christ Jesus. You can confirm for yourself the authenticity of this statement; you can check this out by observing Christians around you whom you considered as faithful Christians, for instance, the church leaders in your local assembly. You can take steps to ask them personal questions to confirm whether it's true or not.

The ignorance of looking down on the Lord's Table must stop forthwith; rather brethren, most especially the young adults should wake up to this reality and responsibility. Most of the time when the brother or sister, feels weak and down, the first thought that comes to mind is how to go and get some medication; no, this is absolutely wrong. The first thing should be to go the Lord's Table and take the communion with the lord Himself. Yes, you can administer the Lord's Supper to yourself with the confines of your home. Call on the name of the lord Jesus Christ; confess that sin(s) to Him, and raise the bread or flake and any non-alcoholic wine up to Him to bless them, and then make some declarations and some prayer points. After that, you can eat the bread and drink the wine in an honorable, respectful, and worthy manner.

BIBLICAL QUOTES WHICH SUPPORTS EATING/DRINKING CHRIST FLESH AND BLOOD.

THE IMPORTANCE OF THE LORD'S SUPPER.

As the feast of Passover was being celebrated, the lord Jesus re-titled it as the Last Supper, and at the birth of the New Testament church the Apostles re- titled again as the Lord's Supper. The lord took bread and gave thanks to God almighty. While He broke the bread and gave it out to His disciples, He made a statement, "This is my flesh given for you; do this always in remembrance of me. "So also, in the same manner, when the supper was finished He held out the cup, speaking, "This cup is the new covenant in my blood, which is poured out for you." – Luke 22:19-21. KJV.

All the accounts of the lord's supper in the synoptic gospels are found in Matthew 26;26-29; Mark 14:17-25; Luke 22:7-22; and in the book of John 13:21-30.Also in 1 Corinthians 11: 23-29, Paul the apostle in respect of the lord's Supper in which He included some particular statements which are not found in the gospels: "Therefore whoever eats the bread and drinks the cup of the lord in an unworthy manner, will be guilty of sinning against the body and blood of the lord. " Everybody should examine himself before attempting to eat this bread and drink from this cup. If any man dares to eat and drink without proper recognition of the lord's body, he has already judged himself.

In 1Corinthians 11:26, Paul made another statement which is also in the synoptic gospels, "For whenever you eat this bread and drink this cup, you proclaim the lord's death until He comes." From the illustration so far, you can understand why the lord Jesus Christ used bread and wine as symbols of His body and blood to establish a great monument of His death. In His declaration He said, the depicts His body that would be broken, and the wine depicts His blood that would be poured out; which is an indicator that He was going to experience a terrifying death very soon.

And then He said, "Do this in remembrance of me.", indicating that the ceremony should be continue to be observed in the future till He returns. It also indicates the fulfillment of the scriptures by instituting the Lord's Supper; the Passover lamb which was requested for the sacrifice, and the coming of the Lamb of God who took away the sin of the entire world. By token of the establishment of the Lord's Supper the old covenant was replaced by a new covenant when Christ the Passover Lamb was sacrificed. The old sacrificial system became obsolete and the Lord's Supper or communion table is observed in remembrance of the acts of Christ on our behalf, and celebrates the blessings which resulted from His sacrificial death.

These statements written in the gospels and the book of John are of great importance because they proceeded out of the mouth of the lord Himself and further re-echoed by Paul the apostle; the authenticity of these words cannot be over-emphasized, and so when He said in John 6:51, "I am the living bread which came down from heaven: if any man eat of this bread, he shall live forever: and the bread that I will give is my flesh, which I will give for the life of the world. He meant exactly what He has said.

Today we eat the flesh and drink the blood as symbolized in the bread and wine, for healings, deliverances, and eternal life; any man who eats this flesh and drinks this blood will never die again, rather he will live forever, he will not be sick again as most people do.

POWERFUL PRAYER POINTS

YOUR DECLARATION:

"And they overcame him by the blood of the Lamb, and by the Word of their testimony; as a weapon." - Revelation 12:11. KJV.

In the mighty name of Christ Jesus, I am truly a born-again child of the most high God. I trust and have faith in God the father, as well as Christ Jesus His son, and the blessed Holy Spirit who fills me up from the inside. I fully trust and believe in the immovable powerful Word of God.

This is what I believe:

- That life and death are in power of my tongue.
- That this confession I make today with the power in my tongue, shall be into life.
- That I shall prosper according to the Words which the lord has this day put in my mouth.

As it is written "Whoso eateth my flesh, and drinketh my blood, hath eternal life; and I will raise him up at the last day. For my flesh is meat indeed, and my blood is drink indeed. He eateth my flesh, and drinketh my blood, dwelleth in me, and I in him." --John 6:54, 55. Lord, with firm faith in my mind I stretch forth my arm with this cup of your blood (Lamb of God) and I consume it, and I will possess eternal life.

Let the blood of Christ quicken every dead thing within me; and let the strength of my life be resurrected by the blood. Let the blood invigorate, revitalize, remold and revive every buried abilities and gifts of the Holy Spirit within me. Every inherited self-damaging demonic deposit in my body, be flushed out. Let the blood of Christ purify my spiritual and physical blood circulating systems. Let the blood of Christ transform everything in my life to become anew.

My lord Jesus, please make me drunk with your blood and I shall be filled with eternal life. It is written, "Be strong in the Lord and in the power of His might." My father and my lord, I request that you become my very might and strength each day of my life. Father, do not allow me to fall into the traps of my enemies and the praise of your name will never depart from my mouth all the days of my life. With my heart I truly believe the Word of God in my heart and with my mouth I have made this confession unto salvation. Lord Jesus, performed unto me as I have prayed according to your word, in Christ Jesus wonderful and gracious name. Amen.

KEEP SILENT FOR 5-10 MINUTES.

(Listen to the Holy Spirit).

- I release the power in the covenant blood of Christ Jesus to revive every dead things in my life.
- I release the power in the covenant blood of Christ Jesus to arrest every strong man of my father's house.
- I release the power in the covenant blood of Christ Jesus to arrest every strong man of my mother's house.

- I plead the covenant blood of Christ Jesus upon my spirit, soul, body, and destiny.
- I apply the covenant blood of Christ Jesus over my house and the whole premises.
- I soak myself in the covenant blood of Christ Jesus.
- I soak my family in the covenant blood of Christ Jesus.
- I soak my business in the covenant blood of Christ Jesus.
- I soak my finances in the covenant blood of Christ Jesus.
- I dipped my destiny in the covenant blood of Christ three times for a thorough cleaning.
- I dipped my body in the covenant blood of Christ Jesus three times for thorough cleaning of my blood vessels.
- I dipped my marriage in the covenant blood of Christ Jesus against every projection from the Marine kingdom.
- I dipped my children in the covenant blood of Christ Jesus against every attack from witchcraft covens.
- I soak myself in the covenant blood of Christ Jesus against the spirit of delay and frustration.
- I soak myself in the covenant blood of Christ Jesus against the spirit of failure at the gate of success.

CHAPTER FIVE: SHOW-CASE CHRIST BLOOD FOR

(BREAK-THROUGHS IN ALL AREAS OF LIFE).

- ✓ Introduction.
- ✓ The Benefifs Of Christ Covenant Blood.
- ✓ The Power In Christ Covenant Blood.
- ✓ Testimonies Of Power From The Blood Of Jesus.
- ✓ Powerful Prayer Points.

INTRODUCTION.

In any socio-economic system, manufacturers or inventors of goods and services, advertise and promote their products to attract many buyers or consumers. According to the lord Jesus Christ, "No man when he had lighted a candle, putteth it in a secret place, neither under a bushel, but on a candlestick, that they which come in may see the light." – Luke 11:33 KJV. Nobody who produced a unique product and would take it and hide it away from people so that it will not be sold; rather he will polish it and make it attractive for the consumer to buy it. He will back it up with much advertising and promotional campaign in other to have more sales.

One of the reasons why this book is written is to show-case the enormous power embedded in the blood of Jesus Christ, but the church is reluctant to let the world know this; we have been drawn away into too much religion and we forgotten the real purpose why Christ came to this world. Jesus has come firstly to rescue man from sin, and secondly to wrestle power (authority) from the hands of Satan and restore it back to man; and this cannot be done without real fight against Satan. Jesus Christ used His blood to conquer Satan and took from him all his weapons of war; they are: SIN (anger, violence, hatred, malice, murder, adultery, fornication, sicknesses, diseases, sexual perversion, bestiality, materialism) and death. By this singular blood of Jesus Christ Satan was woefully defeated, disarmed and kept under your feet, along with his cohorts; this is the message we must not keep to ourselves alone.

There are too many benefits accruing to the blood of Christ, for instance, forgiveness, justification, spared from God's wrath, spiritual healing, spiritually alive, conscience alive, spiritually cleansed, peace with God, power to overcome evil, no longer cursed, no longer condemned, redeemed, covenant child of promise, translated into God's kingdom, God's unmerited favor, declared righteous, close to God, joint heir with Christ, I am free, protected 24/7, separated from the world, victorious, bold & confident to enter into the holy of holies, aligned with God; these and many more benefits are at your disposal only and only if you can simply understand what the covenant blood of Jesus Christ really mean to you. Believe this and there will be no need to be afraid of Satan and demons anymore.

THE BENEFITS OF CHRIST COVENANT BLOOD.

I am sure you are aware of the millions of benefits accruable to the covenant blood of the lord Jesus Christ. As a young Christian with simple faith in Christ, knows that virtually everything we need to do on this planet earth, we will need the blood of Jesus Christ as a cover or shield before we can successfully accomplish our various tasks without compromising, because our enemy, the accuser of the brethren is always at the corner to cause to worship or acknowledge him before you can do anything. As you carry out your daily activities you need the blood of the Christ for cover and you do not have to bow down your head to Satan before you do what you want to do.

Truly, there is power in the covenant blood of Jesus Christ, and I think it's time for the entire body of Christ to wake up and let the world know about the inherent power in the blood, making everyone understand that it is not an ordinary blood.

Here are some few benefits of the covenant blood of Christ Jesus that you should receive and appropriate by faith.

FIVE GREAT BENEFITS OF CHRIST COVENANT BLOOD.

THE BLOOD PROTECTS US.

The blood of the Passover lamb saved the children of Israel from being destroyed by the spirit of death in Egypt; so also, Jesus Christ, the lamb of God takes away death from anyone who puts his trust in Him, as well as full protection from sicknesses, ailments, diseases, poverty, curses, evil Covenants, bondage, and sin. - 1 Corinthians 5:7.

THE BLOOD DELIVERS US FROM BONDAGE.

> *"And they overcame him by the blood of the Lamb and by the word of their testimony; and they love not their lives unto the death." – **Revelation 12:11.***

To overcome Satan you need to testify personally against Satan and as you do so, the blood of Jesus will begin to do the miraculous for you. You cannot keep your mouth shut and expect miracles or wonders taking place.

The blood of Jesus purchased (the blood was the currency used for the purchase), and restored our authority; and deliverance from every power that has held us captive. The blood destroys addictions, destroys spiritual bondages, and stops every work of darkness perpetuated by the enemy. When we continue to preach the Word of God and keep testifying about the power in the covenant blood of Jesus, we are exercising our faith and authority over the works of Satan, and at the same time getting delivered from power of demonic forces and influence. Whatever the enemy has done previously in your life are automatically reversed by the innate power of the blood of Christ Jesus.

THE BLOOD HEALS US.

As earlier mentioned the blood of Jesus is the currency that was used to purchase your freedom totally from the hands of Satan, and your divine healing, divine health, and forgiveness are inclusive. Read Isaiah 53:5.

THE BLOOD GIVES PEACE.

I am a living testimony of the peace that only God can give. The world and every luxury in it cannot give you that peace which only God can give. The Lord Jesus said, "Peace I leave with you, my peace I give unto you: not as the world giveth, give I unto you. Let not your heart be troubled, neither let it afraid." That's the secret thing the covenant blood of Christ released into our hearts which we are enjoying but an outsider will never understand.

THE BLOOD GIVES RIGHTEOUSNESS.

We must go out there to tell them about these things; let's not talk about physical miracles alone. The journey to receive the peace of mind from the Lord Jesus begins with a thorough cleaning job of our conscience with the blood of Jesus. When our conscience is fully washed and cleansed from every guilt, He releases His peace; He is the one that gives it there. Once we have made everything right with God, then we have the peace. Read Romans 5:1.

THE POWER IN CHRIST BLOOD.

For a very long time men used animal sacrifices to cover up their sins, but could not wipe it out so that God would not see it again; animal blood could nod not erase the of sins of man. The sins man commit irritates God, they needed to be erased. Only the blood of Christ Jesus could pacify God, so man needed the blood of Christ Jesus, as soon as it was done, God's anger was abated; man's sin was forgiven and God was reconciled with man to continue from where the communion fellowship stopped when Adam disobeyed God's command.

You need to understand these stories in the simplest form so that you can get a clear picture of the jig saw and imbibe the importance. It was a day's journey from heaven to earth for the purpose of this great 'ones and for all' sacrifice; and since the time the sacrifice was concluded, any man or woman who comes to

Jesus Christ for repentance and forgiveness of sin, was duly forgiven and the sin wiped off automatically.

Through the blood of Jesus Christ man receives healing to his spirit, soul, and body. The blood heals every type of sicknesses and diseases because the scripture says, "…His stripes we are healed…" Also we obtain deliverance from all manner of human affliction through the blood of Christ. There are many who are captive of the mighty (devil). Now, no matter how mighty that devil might be, there is no spiritual battle, warfare, or combat that has the power to withstand the blood of Jesus Christ. Anywhere the name of Christ Jesus is mentioned, all knees must bow, of things in heaven, earth, or underneath the earth. That is how powerful the is. Every work of Satan and his cohorts are dislodged by the blood of Jesus Christ; the blood of Christ is dreaded by Satan and his cohorts.

There is nothing the believer needed more than the covenant blood of Christ Jesus to conquer the enemy and obtain your victory. When life deals blow at you, just run to the Jesus and plead His blood. Every problem of life, every challenges of life, every difficulty in life you are faced with right now, will submit easily the moment you plead the blood of Jesus Christ. When you develop the attitude to participate in communion tables, you will learn very fast how the blood of Christ Jesus speaks; salvation, forgiveness, freedom, blessing, abundant life, peace, healings, deliverance, etc.

TESTIMONIES ABOUT THE BLOOD OF JESUS CHRIST.

Dear Rev,

Greetings in the name of our Lord and Savior. I was suffering from a blood disease, typhoid and a fungal disorder which causes cancer. I wrote you with my prayer request. Now, I am completely healed!

Thank you very much for the blest cloth and magazine you sent to me. I keep them in my bag wherever I go. Though I called myself a Christian, I was not really saved. Now, I quit smoking, drinking, and I am a free person. Thank you once again for praying for me for my sickness. May the Lord use you to do many mighty works.

Yours lovingly,

Chennai, South India

Dear Rev,

While reading [your Giant Little Book] "The Whipping Post," and praying your prayers, I felt the discomfort in my shoulder, which was broken from being hit by a van, go away. I also felt healing in my head. Also, all the other damage still evident and other problems, such as arthritis, bone soreness, soft tissue damage, etc. is gone. I had epilepsy after an earlier car accident in 1972, and it is also healed.

Victoria, British Columbia,

Dear Rev

Greetings and many thanks for the prayers that you and your prayer warriors have prayed and are still offering to the Most High God on my behalf. It gladdened my heart that our God has brought you to us through our Lord Jesus. I am so blessed to receive letters of encouragement and the magazines. I live every day and night praising and rejoicing in the Lord. Something wonderful happened in my life, and I know that the Lord has made me whole. All my problems and troubles are gone.

The blest cloth has delivered not only me but also my cousin's brother who was ill with a nonstop headache and swollen legs. I prayed with him believing that the blood of Jesus will heal. He is now healthy and fit. Jesus our Lord is still fighting the battles for us, and He has won the victory. Rev, I love you and all your prayer warriors; you are all special to us.

Yours in Christ,

Itsoseng, South Africa

Dear Rev.,

I want to thank you for the blest cloth because it has brought about total deliverance for many people in two cities. Hundreds have been saved and healed through your teachings and the blest cloth.

The strongest testimony is about my uncle who was given a very dangerous poison. He was taken to one of the biggest hospitals in Uganda and then on to Zambia, but the doctors told me that all the intestines were damaged and that he would not be well again. Since there was nothing they could do for him, I discharged him from the hospital to bring him back home. Still, I couldn't believe he would die; and my heart said, "When I call on Jesus, everything is possible."

When we reached home, I received a letter from you; and there I found the blest cloth. I told my uncle, "I have a Doctor who can heal your sickness." I pinned the blest cloth to his shirt; and after that, I poured water in a cup and dropped pieces of the cloth inside. I gave him the water to drink, and I knew right then that the power of God was moving in his body like a holy, burning fire.

Within two days, I saw that he was a different person; and he even told me, "I will not die!" He is thanking God for using you to heal and deliver him. Now, the song in my heart is from Psalm 98:1, **O sing unto the LORD a new song; for he hath done marvelous things: his right hand, and his holy arm, hath gotten him the victory.** May God bless you and your ministry.

Katakwi, Uganda

Dear Rev.

I thank God for the letter you sent full of blessings and answers to my needs. I asked you to send me the blest cloth, and I received it. From that time, I have seen so many miracles; and I told you that I had a problem with chest pain and about my father having a problem with leg pains. Let me tell you what the Lord did—we are all healed.

One Sunday, I was preaching in another area; and there was a pastor who was not hearing. The blest cloth was in my pocket, and I motioned to him that God was going to heal him. Then I touched his ears, and our Lord Jesus gave him his hearing. After he received his miracle, he testified to the people at church.

Yours in Christ,

Lilongwe, Malawi

Dear Rev. Angley,

I would like to share my testimony with you. The backache I complained about has healed. I can now bend and even carry my grandchild on my back, and I don't feel pains. Thank you, Jesus. I praise Him. Also, I could not use my right thumb. It was so painful that I couldn't open it even a little to carry a drink. I prayed and wrapped it with my blest cloth, and a miracle happened. My thumb healed, and I am able to write again and use it well. Jesus has healed me. I thank Him so much for this wonderful miracle.

I pray that God will shower you with blessings every day for the wonderful work you do for millions of people. I pray for you and your team.

Thanking Jesus,

Barkly East, Eastern Cape, South Africa

Dear Rev.,

We want to share with you a miracle healing through the blest cloth you sent. We were evangelizing and met a lady who could only see a distance of a meter (3 ft.). She came to the meeting we held in the Ngesumini village. We prayed for her and put the blest cloth on her eyes as we laid hands on her. A miracle happened, and her sight was restored. Now, it seems that she can see even a mile away!

In the same meeting and using the same blest cloth, a girl came whose leg was two inches shorter than the other. After praying and laying the blest cloth on her short leg, it was lengthened to the size of the other instantly! She is no more limping.

Both sisters gave their lives to Jesus and attend church, testifying of how they received their miracles. Glory to God! May the grace of our Lord Jesus be with you as you serve Him faithfully.

Litein, Kenya

Dear Rev.

My husband was on a kidney dialysis machine because his kidney had stopped working. I called your prayer line; and the next day, his kidney started working. I thank God for what He did, and I thank you for your prayers.

Warren, Ohio, USA

Dear Rev,

I called the prayer line for arthritis in my back. I could not lie down in bed at night. The lady prayed with me and said, "Now, go to bed." I said, "I will." I have had no more pain when I lie down from that night on.

Donegal, Pennsylvania, USA

Dear Rev.,

I want to thank God for you and your ministry. Immediately when I received your first letter in late August, things changed in my life and in the lives of my family. My mum, who has been oppressed and sick for many years, received healing; God has given her a sound mind. Love has been restored in my family, and my father is looking to God for help.

My stepmother's witchcraft is powerless. My brother was leading an immoral life and was a chain smoker. He has stopped smoking, and he is changing for the good. I was coughing persistently; but when I received the blest cloth, I was healed immediately. I was also healed of ulcers. When I would eat my food, my stomach was in such pain until I would vomit everything out; but God healed me!

Our lives have ceased paining. May God bless you, and may His hand be continually upon you. You have been such a blessing to so many, especially to my family members; your prayers have touched them. Last but not least, God is removing me from the pit of debt.

Thanks,

Nakuru, Kenya

Dear Rev.

I received your letter and blest cloth. Before I knew about your ministry, I used to be very sick; but nowadays I am fine—no ulcers, eyes problems, high blood pressure or swollen legs. I can do my work as usual.

In my area, people do not pray; they believe in going to witch doctors and those teaching occult practices. There are many divorces, crimes and dirty things which do not please Jesus. People go to church but do not worship God in their hearts.

I am happy that I am saved by Jesus who healed all my diseases from my whole body and showed me miracles. I wake up every day at 3AM to pray. I pray for your ministry and love it very much. May Jesus bless you.

Yours in Jesus' name,

Turbo, Kenya

God's Miracle Power Destroys AIDS

Dear Rev.

I want to thank you from the bottom of my heart for your great support and the prayers offered for me. I have received several miracles, one of which is the greatest miracle I've ever known or seen. I give God all the glory regarding my life. The idea for "establishing" a blest cloth brings Jesus into an arena He has never been in before, and it's all for one purpose—sharing God's Word in the most effective way.

After receiving the blest cloth, I spent more time in prayers. Three days later, I received my healing; and the Holy Ghost started speaking through me in tongues as He gave the utterance. I am no longer a victim of AIDS, ulcers and hypertension. I have enclosed my photo for this testimony.

Kitale, Kenya

Dear Rev,

I greet you in the name of the Lord Jesus. I want to thank our Lord for His love for us through you, Man of God. I want to share this testimony about a certain sister who was suffering from AIDS. She was critical and had even stopped talking and was taken to the hospital. Her family called me to come and pray for her.

I went there; and when I saw the condition of this sister, I asked myself, "Lord, how shall I pray?" Jesus told me that I was to just pin the blest cloth to her gown and pray. A year later, this same sister is back to life and healthy. She intends to now join our church because she has seen the real power of God. Blest cloths are important here as our point of contact with God. God has really anointed you, Rev. Angley. God bless you.

Nyimba, Zambia

Dear Rev.,

I greet you in the name of our Lord, Jesus Christ. I was diagnosed HIV positive in 2006. I wrote requesting for prayers, and you sent me a blest cloth. Through your prayers and faith in God, I am here to confess that I have been healed. Thanks to the Lord for such a great miracle!

I also requested prayer for my elder sister who was HIV positive and my younger sister who was epileptic. Both sisters are healed! Through your prayers, there is peace in our family—something I was asking God for.

As I read through your magazine, I have gained true salvation. May the Almighty God bless your work as you support the body of Christ.

Your friend in Christ,

Kipkaren River, Kenya

Dear Rev.

I am a widow with two children. It was a miracle when I witnessed a relative's son cured of AIDS through the blest cloth which you sent to him in 2006. May the Lord keep you blessed with many years.

Dear Rev. Thank you for the wonderful letter and blest cloth. Me and my family wrote asking for prayers since I was HIV/AIDS positive, and my health had deteriorated to such a degree that many people and friends counted me off. But our Lord and Master is great, and now people wonder whether they are really seeing me or someone else. I am the talk of the town of how God performs wonders and what He does.

Truly, He is our help for soul, mind and body. I am well. Praise God! In Him, I now live. I am living happily and thank you again for the magazines, The Power of The Holy Ghost. They are great. I share them with my friends.

Thank you,

Masvingo, Zimbabwe

Dear Rev,

I would like to greet you in the name of the Lord. I am so happy for all that has happened to us as a family. I would like to let you know that the blest cloth you sent, I divided into four because I was surrounded by some sick people; and God is great. I happened to know the truth about God's miracle power, so I was able to share with them.

One lady became blind after giving birth, and then the baby died. When she became blind, it saddened everyone in our town because she is commonly known. One Sunday, I went to church carrying the blest cloth so that I could tell her about it. After the service, I approached her; and she was very happy to be told about God's love. I told her about miracles through the blood of Jesus by His chosen man, Rev. Angley. She never heard of such a thing. I prayed for her and pinned the piece of blest cloth to her clothing. In some few days, the person staying with her told my wife that she had started seeing. Praise the Lord Jesus!

God has made me a different man because of *The Power of The Holy Ghost* magazines. I went for my CD4 count which before was only 105 (which means death), but today the test showed it to be 516. God is a miracle-working God, and He healed me of the HIV virus! God bless you and the ministry so much.

Maralal, Kenya

Dear Rev.

I want to take this opportunity to thank God for healing me from the HIV virus. Last year, I presented my request for healing from

AIDS, and you sent me a blest cloth. Since then, the virus has been undetectable; and my CD4 count has risen from 250 to 589.

Hampshire, United Kingdom

Dear Rev.,

Praise be unto God who chose you, Rev, to do His wonderful work. I used to write letters to you and you sent me magazines. I enjoyed reading them a lot, but I was still in sin—I was in love with a married man. Last year, I went to have my blood tested; and I found out that I was HIV positive.

Something came into my mind that I needed to confess my sins and give my life to Jesus. I knew I could have victory in the precious name of Jesus. I had one of your books, The Reality of the Blood, so I went to that book. The Holy Spirit touched me, and I felt something very strange. I had a feeling that, through the teachings in that book, I am going to be healed. Although I had the book for some time, it was the first time I opened it to read it. After reading, I confessed all my sins, praying and holding the book as if I was holding to God's hand. I learned a lot about the blood of Jesus.

I went back to have my blood tested again, and a miracle happened—I tested negative! I believe in the miracle power of God; and since I have read your magazines, I have more of God's divine knowledge and wisdom. I will live a clean, pure life with Jesus because my body is the temple of God. I have made my final choice, and I am going to serve God. I know the Word of God is my mirror to show me just what kind of person I really am. Rev, I love you and your ministries very much.

Yours in Christ,

Taung Station, South Africa

Dear Rev. I count it a blessing when you replied to my letter and gave me a blest cloth. When I received the blest cloth, I put my faith together with yours. It was on December 17, 2009 that the miracle happened. After I received your reply, I immediately went for the blood test on January 22, 2010.

Later, I was called to the health clinic for the results. To my surprise, I was told that my CD4 count was 347 and the viral load was 0-40, which means that it is undetectable; and the virus was not seen in my blood. An HIV positive report is nothing before God. As you wrote in your letter to me, "It's not within man to do miracles but to believe the true and living God."

I thank God for giving you the strength and power to pray over the blest cloth and then send it to me along with such an encouraging letter. I am healed through faith in God, and I am prepared to give my testimony at the church this coming weekend. I will keep on praying to the living God. I thank God for everything that has happened to me within a short period of time.

Yes, God is so wonderful. He will never fail His children. I also ask you to print my testimony as I have sent also my photo so that I can glorify His name. God bless you and multiply your days in order to fulfill His work.

Yours—Healed!

Makhado, South Africa

Jesus Is Our Healer

Dear Rev.

I have a wonderful miracle to report to you. A short while back, my mother and I came up on the platform to receive prayer for my grandmother who lives in Clarksburg, West Virginia and was diagnosed with bladder cancer. Although my grandmother did not come, my mother brought her picture as a point of contact; and you laid hands on the picture and agreed with us for her deliverance.

Afterwards, they took my grandmother to the clinic for evaluation; and after the scope test, they told my grandmother that as far as they are concerned she is cancer-free! To God be all the honor, praise, glory and power! Not only is she cancer-free, but her bladder is in wonderful condition! It's just like Jesus to do this for my grandma! I love Him, and I love and thank you for believing with us and for your words of encouragement during that time. God is a good God!

Akron, Ohio, USA

Dear Rev. I greet you, Pastor, and your ministry in the name of Jesus. Thank you for sending the blest cloth. I requested it for my daughter who was suffering from asthma. She is healed completely!

I thank God for giving us somebody like you at this point in time. May the Lord bless you.

Mabopone, South Africa

Dear Rev.

First of all, receive my warm and tender greetings in the name of our Lord and Savior Jesus Christ. I am very glad to share three miracles which occurred in my family after using the blest cloth. First, my brother, aged 27, was deaf in one ear since age 14. I dipped the blest cloth in water and dropped some of the water in his ear. He then attached the cloth to his shirt after a prayer. Within no time, his ear was opened; and now he is using both ears.

Secondly, my in-law, Agnes, was having problems eating beef or goat meat. She would experience some rashes and swelling of the lips whenever she ate meat. She soaked the blest cloth in water and drank the water. She then attached the cloth to her blouse after a prayer of faith. Now, she is able to eat beef and goat meat without any complications—no more rashes and swelling of the lips.

Lastly, my daughter, Martha, had eye problems. After soaking the blest cloth in water, dropping some of the anointed water in her eyes and making a prayer, her eyes have been restored. Really, Jesus is still healing people today. May the Lord give you a long life to continue winning lost souls and attending to the afflicted.

Yours in Christ,

Zomba, Malawi

Dear Rev.

The Lord Jesus is wonderful, and I praise His holy name. I am alive in Jesus and encouraged very much. The blood of Jesus is powerful! I am completely healed from diabetes. I believed, asked the Lord to take away all the pains from my body, and Jesus healed me. The continuous pains and diseases in my body went away. My blood sugar level is very normal. I praise my Jesus!

Thanks, Reverend, for stressing the blood love of Jesus. Thanks for your encouraging letters and magazines. My family is happy, and we are all under the blood.

My 18-year-old daughter's spine disk slipped recently as she was jumping, and she suffered with severe pain. We planned to take her for an x-ray, but she claimed the blood of Jesus as she prayed. At the time, I was away from the home; but the blood power washed all her pain away. She is fine, and we are praising the Lord for healing her. Thanks again for serving us the Master.

Your Sister in the Lord,

Kampala, Uganda

Dear Rev

I came to Grace Cathedral and went into the healing line and received my healing. I had been diagnosed with cancer and was led to your ministry after watching the Sunday telecast we get here. I praise and thank God for my healing, and I am grateful to you for laying hands on the sick that they may recover. I used to take a lot of morphine for pain, but I found I didn't need it and forgot to take it at all. Praise the Lord; healing is the children's bread.

Thank you for having a healing ministry and for your dedication to the Lord that He can use you in this marvelous way.

In Him,

North Vancouver, British Columbia, Canada

Dear Rev.,

I greet you in the name of our Lord Jesus Christ. I would like to thank the Lord for healing me. I had bad sores between my toes for two years. It has been so painful; but this year I said, "Enough is enough of this disease!" I phoned your prayer line and someone in your ministry prayed for me.

Thank God because all the sores have dried, and the itching is gone as well. I know that when we have faith and believe, nothing is too hard for the Lord. I know our God is a mighty God, and He is faithful and wonderful. He promised to never forsake, leave or forget us. God bless you all.

Westcliffon-Sea, England

Dear Rev,

Greetings in the name of my Lord, Jesus. I would like to thank you for your wonderful prayers that have come into effect. I have been praising the Lord ever since 2006 started because my life is not the same. God has really changed my life. I have left things behind that were defiling the temple of God. Previous to my incarceration, I was having an affair for three years. I confessed all my sins, and God forgave me. That sin and stumbling block is gone, and I am now Spirit-filled and serving the Lord.

After I was diagnosed with TB last year, I prayed that I must be healed; and the Bible told me that all diseases come from the devil and not from God. In order to be able to claim my healing, I had to stay right with Him. I fasted every Wednesday and sometimes Thursday, and now I am healthy without any treatments.

Two other inmates and I have started a prayer group; and it is growing in number, and it is so powerful. We are telling others about the importance of confessing all your sins and leaving them.

Also, my son was not behaving properly and was quite mischievous, but he is all right again. Your prayers are really blessing me. May God bless you at all times.

Yours in Christ Jesus,

East London, South Africa

Dear Rev.

Thank you very much for the three separate posts you sent. After reading the magazine, I became bold in the Lord Jesus and believed that there is nothing beyond the reach of God. I have read the tracts about the Holy Spirit, and now I am reading *Untying God's*

Hands. I am happy that at the time when I needed a friend to comfort me, you encouraged and strengthened me in the Lord.

Last week, I saw my son, who had been unable to walk, taking many steps. I knew it was your prayers that made it happen in the name of Jesus. Since I started receiving literature from you, I have been able to secure a room for myself. I thank you for all you have done for me.

I pray that God will give you a long life and bless your work so that the name of Jesus will spread to every corner of the world. It is my strongest desire to know much about the Holy Ghost and the work of Jesus. God has saved my son, who is just three years old, from total paralysis.

Affectionately and faithfully yours,

Kumasi, Ghana

Dear Rev.,

Thank you for your prayers, for your letter and the book, The Deceit of Lucifer. I am no longer a fortuneteller for I now know the truth. I have suffered for five years. I left school because I was sick, and demons forced me into fortunetelling. I did not know anything about the power in the blood of Jesus. I did not know that we are living in a very dangerous world, ignorant and deceived about God.

The Lord has opened His promises to me. I even felt His very powerful presence as I read the promises from the Bible. One time I was sick, and I thought that I would never be well again. I had pains in my spinal cord and also in my chest; but while I was pleading the blood of Jesus, God was healing me. I put my hands on my back, and a miracle happened! I was instantly healed and have no back pain. Praise God! God bless you.

Your friend in the Lord,

Norlim, South Africa

Dear Rev.

I greet you in the name of Jesus Christ. I received your books and your blest cloth that you have prayed over. I pinned the cloth inside my clothing as you had instructed me and believed God to get me well. I am glad to let you know that the power and anointing of God through Jesus Christ came upon me because I went to the doctor, and he said that I have no sickness anymore.

I was troubled with diabetes and blood pressure problems. I received my miracles after suffering for some five years. I thank the Lord of glory for His anointed gifts which work in you mightily. I thank the Lord and praise Him for healing me.

Yours faithfully,

Nickerie, Suriname

Divine Miracles Are for Today

Dear Rev,

Thank God for your great help. I have been suffering from malaria and joint pain for about one year. As a result, it has made me become so lazy at doing my work and going to church. One day, I happened to meet with a brother in Christ who helped me very much. He fed me with God's Word first which actually comforted my heart; and after that, he gave me a piece of a blest cloth that I put in a glass of water and then drank the water. After a short period, I felt some great changes in my body and my soul; and I was totally healed!

Now, I do go to church every Sunday, and also I do all my daily work very well. The reason is I have received some new strength in my life. Also, now I am newly transformed by the blood of Jesus Christ. Thank you very much, Servant of God. May the Lord bless you together with your ministry workers. Hallelujah!

Yours faithfully,

Busia, Kenya

Dear Rev.,

On a Saturday afternoon, I called your prayer line for my minister who had cancer on his nose. When I greeted him the next morning at church, his nose looked well. I could see no sign of the cancer. As we shook hands, he said, "I was walking into a store yesterday afternoon, and the cancer just fell off." Our God is an awesome God!

Piedmont, Alabama, USA

Dear Rev

The Lord is good to my family, and every day with Jesus is sweeter than the day before. Last year, I wrote a letter requesting prayer for me, my brother and my cousin. My cousin and I had problems with our ears; they were bleeding. My brother had lung problems and high blood pressure.

Thank you for your prayers because all of us received God's healing. I thank the blood name of Jesus. May God bless you, your ministry and your family.

Mabopane, South Africa

Dear Rev.

I am born again and have read some of your sermons. I especially loved this one—*Thirty Bible Reasons Why You Must Have the Holy Ghost to Make the Rapture*. I spent some weeks reading this sermon and trying to grasp the theme until the Holy Spirit helped me to understand. From that time, I was thirsty for the Holy Ghost baptism; I needed His baptism.

During the course of a night as I was alone in my room, I was devoted to prayer. It was around 1AM. Suddenly, something, which never happened to me before, took place—I spoke a different language which I never knew! The power of the Holy Ghost "troubled" my tongue, and thereafter it was awesome.

I know I have the baptism of the Holy Ghost! I have learned a lot, and I'm continuing to become rooted and grounded in the Word of God. I want to lift Jesus, and only Jesus, high and share His Gospel. Thank you for your prayers.

Free State, South Africa.

POWERFUL PRAYER POINTS.

YOUR DECLARATION:

*"And they overcame him by the blood of the Lamb, and by the Word of their testimony; as a weapon." - **Revelation 12:11. KJV.**

In the mighty name of Christ Jesus, I am truly a born-again child of the most high God. I trust and have faith in God the father, as well as Christ Jesus His son, and the blessed Holy Spirit who fills me up from the inside. I fully trust and believe in the immovable powerful Word of God.

This is what I believe:

- That life and death are in power of my tongue.
- That this confession I make today with the power in my tongue, shall be into life.
- That I shall prosper according to the Words which the lord has this day put in my mouth.

As it is written "Whoso eateth my flesh, and drinketh my blood, hath eternal life; and I will raise him up at the last day. For my flesh is meat indeed, and my blood is drink indeed. He eateth my flesh, and drinketh my blood, dwelleth in me, and I in him." --John 6:54, 55. Lord, with firm faith in my mind I stretch forth my arm with this cup of your blood (Lamb of God) and I consume it, and I will possess eternal life.

Let the blood of Christ quicken every dead thing within me; and let the strength of my life be resurrected by the blood. Let the blood invigorate, revitalize, remold and revive every buried abilities and gifts of the Holy Spirit within me. Every inherited self-damaging demonic deposit in my body be flushed out. Let the blood of Christ purify my spiritual and physical blood circulating systems. Let the blood of Christ transform everything in my life to become anew.

My lord Jesus, please make me drunk with your blood and I shall be filled with eternal life. It is written, "Be strong in the Lord and in the power of His might." My father and my lord, I request that you become my very might and strength each day of my life. Father, do not allow me to fall into the traps of my enemies and the praise of your name will never depart from my mouth all the days of my life. With my heart I truly believe the Word of God in my heart and with my mouth I have made this confession unto salvation. Lord Jesus, performed unto me as I have prayed according to your word, in Christ Jesus wonderful and gracious name. Amen.

KEEP SILENT FOR 5-10 MINUTES.

(Listen to the Holy Spirit).

DO SOME PRAISE AND WORSHIP.

- Father, in the name of Christ Jesus, I thank you for the great benefits and the provision of the covenant blood of Jesus for me.

- Today, by the covenant blood of Christ Jesus, I proclaim victory over sin, Satan and his cohorts in the name of Jesus.

- I neutralize by the covenant blood of Christ Jesus every stubborn problem in my life and I command them to leave now, in Jesus name.

- I plead the covenant blood of Christ Jesus on every part of my body, including all my internal organs in Jesus mighty name.

- I immerse my destiny in the covenant blood of Christ Jesus in Jesus mighty name.

- I neutralize by the covenant blood of Christ Jesus, every demonic powers sponsored by Satan's agents against me and my family in Jesus name.

- Today, I apply all the available weapons in the covenant blood of Christ Jesus against all the powers sponsored by demons of my father's house, to delay and frustrate my life, in Jesus name.

- By the covenant blood of Christ Jesus, I withstand all the deities of my community assigned to destroy my destiny, in Jesus name.

- I make this declaration today: by the covenant blood of Christ Jesus and the Word of God; SATAN, I AM UNSTOPPABLE in Jesus name. Shout out (7 times).

- By the comprehensive power in the Covenant blood of Christ Jesus, I command every door that I have mistakenly opened to guardian demons, ancestral and familiar spirits from my father and mother's houses to be shut now and forever, in Jesus name.

BEFORE YOU PROCEED, JUST MAKE THIS SIMPLE DECLARATION:

- By the covenant blood of Christ Jesus and word of God, I have been redeemed from the grip of Satan, sin and sorrows; I walk circumspectly in the light of God; I have the Life of God in me; I have access into the presence of God now. Praise God, Hallelujah.
- Every power emanating from curses and Covenants from my father and mother's houses, reversing the works of God in my life, be blotted out now by the covenant blood of Christ Jesus in Jesus name.
- Every power emanating from curses and Covenants from my father and mother's houses, preventing the fulfillment of my destiny, be flushed out now by the covenant blood of Christ Jesus, in Jesus mighty name.
- The blood of Jesus! the blood of Jesus!! the blood of Jesus!!! revive now every part of my life, destiny, and ministry that needs revival in Jesus name.
- The blood of Jesus! the blood of Jesus!! the blood of Jesus!!! Erase, paralyze, and defeat every trace of the work of darkness in my life, destiny, and ministry, in Jesus name.

CONCLUSION.

In Isaiah 49:24 the scripture says, "Shall the prey be from the mighty, or the lawful captive delivered?" This indicates that many people have been lawfully taken prisoners by Satan and his demons; you are a captive because you actually committed sin that makes you to be taken a prisoner of Satan and his demons. Nevertheless, there's hope for you. Now read Isaiah 49:25,"But thus says the lord, Even the captives of the mighty shall be taken away, and the prey of the terrible shall be delivered: for I will contend with him that contendeth with thee, and I will save thy children. God is saying here, even if a demon takes you a prisoner, God says, He will take you back from the hand of that demon, or even if Satan the terrible one holds as a powerless (prey) prisoner; God says, He will deliver you from his hands.

In Isaiah 49:26, "And I will feed them that oppress thee with their own flesh, and they shall be drunken with their own blood, as with sweet wine: ..." This verse is saying to you, though Satan and his demons planned to eat your flesh and drink your blood, they will not be able to do so, instead He will feed Satan and his demons with their own flesh and drink their own blood, but you shall be set free unhurt.

In the physical sense, it is true there are people who drink human blood for whatever reasons; they are called vampires. There is a community of vampires in every city of the world; they know themselves and how they operate. Their operational methods are secretive in nature. Yes, human beings drink human blood and the main reasons according to them are as follows:

- It assists incurring some sicknesses, ailments, and strengthens weak nerves and muscles.
- It invigorates the whole body and gives it a youthful look.
- It revitalizes the human spirit and gives it a spiritual prowess, i.e., empowers the human to become more powerful in the spiritual realm.
- It is the main food for evil spirit beings, including Satan. This occurs when human beings are sacrificed to them and they drink the blood as their food.

Evil spirit beings (demons) cause the death of humans so that they can feed on their blood; and the gullible (sinners) ones become their victims. This was what Isaiah 49:25 was referring to as "captives of the mighty" and "prey of the terrible"

Human agents of darkness, e.g., witches, wizards, herbalists, cultists, marine agents, drink human blood spiritually, except herbalists and cultists that occasionally eat human flesh. They kill humans for the purpose of using the blood:

- To obtain favor from the deities (demons).
- To escape or divert the wrath of the deity (demon).
- To become rich or wealthy.

- To remain in power, or at the top position, to remain a leader.

These wicked evil spirit beings cause a lot of destruction to human lives through many channels such as oppression, depression, obsession, and human affliction. These destructive activities manifest in various forms like tragedies, accidents, disasters, premature deaths, wars, violent crisis, and communal crisis; the result of this, is death for humans which becomes gain for the rulers of darkness of this world. The occurrence of any of the above automatically brings flesh and blood to the dining tables of these wicked spirits.

I have taken time to explain the methods of their operations to you so that you can rise up and stop them. Whatever you are passing through right now, can be traced to evil forces which manipulates humans to their detriment, most especially the ignorant Christians. This is a clarion call for you to rise up and fight. Christ Jesus has given you victory even before you were born; rise up and make use of that victory which is hidden inside the covenant blood of Christ Jesus. The scripture says, "Neither is there salvation in any other: for there is none other name under heaven given among men, whereby we must be saved."

RECOMMENDATIONS.

This book is written and being presented as part 2 of "THE BLOOD: How it works.", also written by the same author, as a follow up; the reason being that the importance, the benefits, and power of the blood of Christ Jesus was not given properly attention hence this one has been written to explain it in fuller details. Both books are recommended to be read at the same time and space together like one indivisible book.

This book could be of great value if the reader makes diligent effort to do the prayers as advised. It is positioned as a self-deliverance manual for everyone who chooses to get out of the grip of Satan our common enemy by proclaiming the covenant blood of Christ Jesus in faith. If you this book religiously, your total deliverance would have been released to you as finished reading the whole book.

YOUR FULL DELIVERANCE IS ASSURED BY THE TIME YOU FINISHED READING THE WHOLE BOOK.

GOD BLESS YOU

www.ingramcontent.com/pod-product-compliance
Lightning Source LLC
Chambersburg PA
CBHW071931120726
48001CB00005B/1939